The Little of Print-making

by Lynne Garner
Illustrations by Marion Lindsay

LITTLE BOOKS WITH **BIG** IDEAS

Featherstone Education
An imprint of Bloomsbury Publishing Plc

50 Bedford Square
London
WC1B 3DP
UK

1385 Broadway
New York
NY 10018
USA

www.bloomsbury.com

Text © Lynne Garner, 2014
Illustrations © Marion Lindsay, 2014
Cover photographs © Shutterstock

British Library Cataloguing-in-Publication Data

A catalogue record for this book is available from the British Library.

ISBN: 978-1-4729-0951-0

Library of Congress Cataloging-in-Publication Data
A catalog record for this book is available from the Library of Congress.

1 3 5 7 9 10 8 6 4 2

Printed and bound in India by Replika Press Pvt. Ltd

This book is produced using paper that is made from wood grown in managed, sustainable forests. It is natural, renewable and recyclable. The logging and manufacturing processes conform to the environmental regulations of the country of origin.

To view more of our titles please visit
www.bloomsbury.com

Contents

Introduction

"Art may seem fun and games — and it is! — but you may not realise that your child is actually learning a lot through exploring the arts and doing art activities. Your children will gain useful life skills when you encourage them to get creative..."

MaryAnn F. Kohl (author, publisher and educational consultant)

www.brightring.com

When encouraging children to enjoy art and craft you are supporting a range of important skills. These are:

Mathematics:

Children are given the opportunity to discuss shape, size and numbers.

Science:

The use of different media allows children to look at concepts such as texture, how things dry, and the mixing of colour.

Economics:

Children not only create 'product' by their efforts, but also become consumers of purchased craft materials. They can also become aware of reducing costs and helping the environment by reusing what would normally be thrown away.

Language:

As children explore arts and crafts, they talk about what they are doing and also look at other children's work, therefore developing their language skills.

Beginning reading:

Whilst creating their art, children will make and read meaningful symbols, e.g. the letters of the alphabet.

Social skills:

In groups, children learn to share materials, co-operate with others and also start to take responsibility in the cleaning up process.

The printing and rubbing techniques outlined in this book use tools and materials that are inexpensive and easy to obtain, and will encourage children to use familiar items in new and exciting ways. As outlined above, the techniques will also help support childrens' educational growth. Each technique is broken down into the following sections:

- ► What you need
- ► What you do (some sections include more than one method)
- ► Tips (where appropriate)
- ► Suggested activities and discussions
- ► Useful links for additional resources
- ► Health and safety tips

In some instances, alternative ideas for materials and tools have been supplied, and additional methods can be found in the 'Useful links for additional resources' sections.

Resources

C. Seinfeld, B.A. Wasik (2006) 'Early Education: Three, Four, and Five Year Olds go to School' (pp166-168)

The early learning goals

When encouraging children to learn through crafting, it is important to support the early years learning goals. This book not only provides step-by-step instructions for how to reproduce each printing technique and suggestions for linked activities, but also provides ideas for discussions that support the revised EYFS framework. The prime and specific areas of the curriculum are broken down into the following seven areas:

Prime areas
▶ Communication and language
▶ Physical development
▶ Personal, social and emotional development

Specific areas
▶ Literacy
▶ Mathematics
▶ Understanding the world
▶ Expressive arts and design

The techniques, activities and discussions included in this book aim to fulfil all seven areas of the EYFS.

Communication and language (CL)

Listening and attention
Single-channelled attention. Can shift from one task to a different task if attention is fully obtained – using a child's name helps focus. Is able to follow directions (if not intently focused on own choice of activity). Maintains attention, concentration and sits quietly during appropriate activity.

Understanding
Understands use of objects (e.g. 'What do we use to cut this?'). Listens and responds to ideas expressed by others in conversation and discussion.

Speaking
Uses a variety of questions (e.g. what, where, who). Uses talk to connect ideas, explain what is happening and anticipate what might happen next, and to recall and relive past experiences. Links statements and sticks to a main theme or intention.

Physical development (PD)

Moving and handling
Shows control in holding and using pouring jugs, hammers, books and mark-making

tools. Uses one-handed tools and equipment, e.g. makes snips in paper with child-safe scissors. Uses simple tools to effect changes in materials.

Making relationships
Demonstrates friendly behaviour, initiates conversations and forming good relationships with peers and familiar adults. Explains own knowledge and understanding, and asks appropriate questions of others.

Self-confidence and self-awareness
Expresses own preferences and interests. Can select and use activities and resources with help. Confident to speak to others about own needs, wants, interests and opinions.

Managing feelings and behaviour
Shows understanding and cooperates with some boundaries and routines. Begins to accept the needs of others and can take turns and share resources, sometimes with support from others. Beginning to be able to negotiate and solve problems without aggression, e.g. when someone has taken his or her toy.

Literacy (L)

Reading
Shows interest in illustrations and print in books, and print in the environment. Knows information can be relayed in the form of print.

Writing
Distinguishes between the different marks he or she makes, and sometimes gives meaning to marks as s/he draws and paints.

Mathematics (M)

Numbers
Creates and experiments with symbols and marks representing ideas of number. Beginning to represent numbers using fingers, marks on paper or pictures. Recognise some numerals of personal significance.

Shape, space and measure
Begins to use the language of size. Uses shapes appropriately for tasks. Uses familiar objects and common shapes to create and recreate patterns and build models.

Understanding the world (UW)

People and communities
Remembers and describes special times and events for family or friends. Enjoys joining in with family customs and routines.

Technology
Operates mechanical toys, e.g. turns the dial on a wind-up toy or pulls back on a friction car. Knows that information can be retrieved from computers.

Expressive arts and design (EAD)

Exploring and using media and materials
Experiments with blocks, colours and marks. Explores colour and how colours can be changed. Explores what happens when s/he mixes colours.

Being imaginative
Captures experiences and responses with a range of media such as music, dance and paint and other materials or words. Chooses particular colours to use for a purpose.

As children create and express themselves through art they develop a range of important life skills and will automatically fulfil many of the EYFS outcomes. For example, as they explain what they are doing they are building on their communication and social skills (PSED). When they listen to an adult explaining the techniques of printing and rubbing they are practising their listening and attention skills (CL). Whilst they handle the printing tools and materials they will be improving their handling skills (PD). If they show awareness of health and safety issues when handling tools and materials they will be developing their self-care skills (PD). As they design and create projects that involve letters and numbers they will be building on their literacy and mathematics skills (L and M). During the various printing and rubbing techniques they will encounter themes such as shape, space and size, therefore again building on their mathematics skills (M). If they choose to create items such as gifts and greetings cards they'll be enjoying and participating in family customs (UW). Finally, as they explore shape, colours, patterns and using different materials, they will be gaining skills in expressing themselves through art (EAD).

Source

'Development Matters in the Early Years Foundation Stage (EYFS)', The British Association for Early Childhood Education, www.early-education.org.uk

Hand and feet printing

This technique is a great way of encouraging the children to discuss the sense of touch... so get ready to get creative and just a little covered in paint!

What you need:

- ▶ Poster paint or similar in various colours
- ▶ Paint trays
- ▶ Rollers
- ▶ Aprons
- ▶ Appropriate cover for the work surface
- ▶ Coloured or white paper – A4 or larger

What you do:

1. Pour a little paint into the tray, then roller back and forth to obtain an even cover of paint on the roller.
2. Roller an even layer of paint onto palms or soles of the feet.
3. Press the palm or sole onto the paper and pull up vertically to avoid smudging the print.
4. Place the print to one side and allow it to dry.

Tip!

If you are going to use the print for any of the suggested activities below, ensure there is plenty of blank paper around the print.

Suggested activities and discussions

▶ As the children create their hand or foot prints, encourage them to talk about what they feel as the roller applies the paint to their skin. Is it warm or cold? Is it rough or smooth? Does it tickle? You can also encourage them to talk about the anatomy of their hands and feet, for example, 'little finger', 'ring finger' and 'index finger'.

▶ Encourage the children to be creative with their hand or foot prints once they are dry. For example, a handprint with the fingers splayed out and turned on its side can be turned into a fish, while a handprint with the fingers pointing down can become a jellyfish. Features can be drawn or materials such as googly eyes, pompoms, glitter, etc. can be used.

▶ Why not create a handprint critter? Particularly effective handprint animals include a hedgehog (the prints become the spines) or a peacock (the prints become the tail).

Useful links for additional resources

www.hertshogline.com: click on 'free download', then scroll down for a free print of a hedgehog face.

www.creatingreallyawesomefreethings.com: type 'hand foot print' in the search field for 59 great ideas.

Health and safety tips

▶ Always ensure you use appropriate non-toxic water-based paint.

▶ Check those taking part in the session do not have an allergy to paint.

Printing with fruit and vegetables

There are so many different fruits and vegetables that can be used to create interesting prints. Explore the food we eat by using it to produce a work of art.

What you need:

▶ Fruits or vegetables of your choice (method one)

▶ Large potatoes (method two)

▶ Felt tip pens

▶ Kitchen rolls

▶ Knives

▶ Cookie cutters (method two)

▶ Poster paints or similar in various colours

▶ Rollers and paint trays

▶ Coloured or white A4 paper

What you do:

Method one (any type of fruit or vegetable)

1. Cut the fruit or vegetable in half.

2. Blot the juice from the flat surface using the kitchen roll.

3. Pour a little paint into the tray, then roller back and forth to cover the roller with a thin, even layer of paint.

4. Roller the paint onto the cut surface of the fruit or vegetable, then press onto the paper. Try to ensure you pull up vertically so the print is not smudged.

5. Allow the print to dry before embellishing further.

Method two (potato only)

1. Cut the potato in half and blot the juices using the kitchen roll.

2. Push a cookie cutter into the surface of the potato centrally, pushing approximately 1cm (1/4") into the surface.

3. Cut away the potato around the outside of the cutter.

4. Remove the cutter to leave a raised section.

Tip!

When using a cookie cutter, pick a simple shape that does not have thin sections as these give better results.

Suggested activities and discussions

► Use this technique as a way to introduce the theme of colour. As the children work, encourage them to look at the colour of the fruit or vegetable they are using to print with. Discuss how some fruit/vegetables change colour as they ripen and how some come in various colours, e.g. peppers (red, green and yellow) and apples (green, red/green and red).

► Draw an outline of a basket or a large storage jar, and fill the image with the prints the children create. You could use a long piece of paper as a 'shelf', and fill this shelf with the 'jars' of fruit and vegetables. This can then be used as a backdrop for imaginative play in a shop or on a market stall.

► Explore how the texture of the fruit and vegetables can be used to create something else. For example, the end section of celery can be used to recreate a flower shape, and a pepper sliced in half makes a great tulip print!

► If using method two, you could choose themed cookie cutters (e.g. animals, modes of transport, etc.) and use the prints to create snap cards.

Useful links for additional resources

www.bbc.co.uk/learningzone: type 'clips 9080' in the search field for a short film about printing with fruit and vegetables.

www.activityvillage.co.uk: type 'handprint crafts' in the search field for a library of ideas.

www.wikihow.com/Paint-With-Fruit-and-Vegetables: a step-by-step post showing you how to create stemmed flower prints using fruit and vegetables.

Health and safety tips

▶ As knives will be used for the cutting process, ensure an adult is always present to assist as necessary.

▶ When using cookie cutters, ensure they have a lip along the top edge, as these are more comfortable to push onto – especially for small hands.

Printing with leaves, flowers and grasses

This is a fantastic way of introducing the children to the wonders of the plant kingdom, including concepts such as texture and the structures of plants.

What you need:

Method one

▶ Foliage

▶ Poster paint or similar, in various colours

▶ Paint trays

▶ Foam rollers

▶ Coloured or white A4 paper

▶ Cover for the work surface

▶ Aprons

▶ Crayons (for rubbings)

▶ A5 ply board – one per child

▶ PVA glue

▶ Brushes

What you do:

Method one

1. Place leaves vein-side up and flowers bloom-side up on the work surface, and cover them with a thin layer of paint.
2. Place the leaf or flower paint-side up onto a piece of scrap paper.
3. Take a second piece of paper and place it carefully over the leaf or flower.
4. Gently rub over the surface of the paper, so it comes into contact with the leaf/ flower.
5. Carefully lift the corner and look at the print. If the print is a little faint, carefully replace and rub again.
6. Check again and, if you are happy, remove the paper and place to one side to allow the print to dry.
7. If you wish to print more than one leaf or flower on a sheet of paper then cover as many leaves/flowers in paint as needed and print them at the same time.

Method two

1. Pick some leaves and place them under books (or something flat and heavy) for a couple of hours.
2. Cover the ply board with a thin layer of PVA glue.
3. Randomly place the leaves on the ply board, vein-side up, trying to ensure they lie as flat as possible.
4. If the leaves overlap then apply a little glue to the back of them to ensure they remain in place.
5. Once you are happy with the design, cover the entire surface with a thin layer of PVA glue.
6. Allow the glue to dry fully before using as a printing block, ideally overnight.
7. Once the glue has dried, cover the surface with a thin layer of paint using the foam rollers.
8. Take a piece of paper and place it gently over the block.
9. Rub over the surface of the paper, so it comes into contact with the block.

10. Carefully lift the corner and look at the print. If the print is a little faint, replace and rub again.

11. Check again and, if you are happy, remove the paper and place to one side to allow the print to dry.

> **Tip!**
> Leaves give better results than flowers for method two, as they tend to lie flatter.

Suggested activities and discussions

▶ If you use large leaves with thick veins in method two, you may find these are suitable to create rubbings. Place a piece of thin paper over the top of the block and gently rub with the side of a crayon. Encourage the children to have fun changing colours and experimenting with different leaves and grasses when creating their blocks.

▶ Print lots of different leaves and use them to create a tree-themed wall collage. Perhaps the tree could become a family tree with a different person's name on each leaf. This could be used to discuss and explore family relationships.

▶ As the children print, encourage them to look at the structure of the leaf, flower or grass. If using leaves, why not also discuss the difference between deciduous and evergreen trees and the process leaves go through each autumn. When using grass, you could discuss which animals eat grass.

▶ Encourage the children to look at the size, shape and colour of the foliage they have collected. For example, compare the green of the leaves and get them to describe the different shades. Also look at the shapes and describe them. In the classroom, encourage them to arrange in size or place the same type together.

▶ Whilst collecting the foliage, encourage the children to learn some of the names of the plants they collect.

Useful links for additional resources

www.firstpalette.com: type 'printing' in the search field for a range of print-related ideas.

www-saps.plantsci.cam.ac.uk/trees/: contains a key for identifying British trees and shrubs.

www.woodlands.co.uk: type 'tree species' in the search field for a guide to trees. Contains a useful image of a leaf and its parts.

http://wildflowerfinder.org.uk: searchable database of wild flowers.

Health and safety tips

▶ Check that no-one taking part suffers from any plant-related allergies such as hay fever.

▶ Be aware when picking foliage that some may be harmful if ingested, or may have a surface that could cause a reaction. If you are concerned that reactions may occur then provide suitable protective gloves.

▶ During the picking process, check for insect life. If an insect is living on the leaf then simply don't pick it. This is an ideal opportunity to talk about the importance of insect life, the food chain and bio-diversity.

Cookie cutter printing

Cookie cutters provide a lovely basic shape that can be easily embellished with a range of craft materials such as pompoms, feathers and sequins, to create fun and educational prints.

What you need:

- ▶ Variety of cookie cutters
- ▶ Poster paint or similar, in various colours
- ▶ Flat trays
- ▶ Thin flat sponges
- ▶ Coloured or white A4 paper
- ▶ Rollers (method two)

What you do:

Method one

1. Pour some paint onto a sponge, then fold it in half and squeeze to disperse the paint. Place the sponge into the tray.

2. Press the cookie cutter into the paint-soaked sponge a couple of times to evenly cover the edge with paint.

3. Lift the cookie cutter up and hover over the tray for a moment, to allow any excess paint to drip back onto the sponge.

4. Once the paint has stopped dripping, press the cookie cutter onto the paper and lift vertically to reduce the risk of smudging the print.

5. Allow to dry fully before embellishing.

Method two

1. Pour some paint into a flat tray and roller back and forth to cover the roller with a thin layer of paint.

2. Roller over the edge of the cookie cutter to cover with a thin layer of paint.

3. Press the painted edge of the cookie cutter onto the paper, lifting vertically to reduce the risk of smudging the print.

4. Allow to fully dry before embellishing.

Suggested activities and discussions

▶ Using a large piece of paper (lining paper is ideal for this project), create an entire scene using themed cookie cutters (e.g. an underwater-themed set, which could be combined with the bubble printing technique).

▶ Rather than making a 'clean' print, encourage the children to load the cookie cutter with a slightly thicker coat of paint, then smudge the print by moving it.

▶ Encourage the children to create their own wrapping paper. Support them as they cover a large sheet of paper with cookie prints. Once dry they can add embellishments such as eyes to animals and wheels to cars.

Useful links for additional resources

www.pinterest.com: type 'printing with cookie cutters' into the search field for a wealth of ideas.

www.netmums.com: type 'printing with cookie cutters' into the search field for further inspiration.

Styrofoam printing

Styrofoam sheets are an ideal method for creating printing blocks. To reduce costs, you can use polystyrene that is used to package food.

What you need:

▶ Styrofoam sheets or polystyrene
▶ Blunt pencils or paint brushes
▶ Cookie cutters
▶ Scissors
▶ Coloured or white A4 paper
▶ Paint trays
▶ Rollers
▶ Poster paints or block printing inks
▶ Scrap paper

What you do:

1. If using recycled materials, cut the foam to a workable size (A5 works well).

2. Using the pencil or the handle end of a paintbrush draw a design into the surface of the foam sheet.

3. Alternatively, push a cookie cutter 2-3mm into the surface of the sheet to create your design.

4. Once the design is complete, cover the surface of the foam sheet with a thin layer of paint or ink using the roller.

5. Place the foam sheet face-up, then carefully place the piece of paper over it and cover with a piece of scrap paper.

6. Using a clean roller, work back and forth over the foam printing-block, ensuring the entire surface of the block comes into contact with the paper.

7. Remove the scrap paper, then carefully pull off the printed paper to reveal the completed design.

8. Place to one side to allow the print to dry.

> **Tip!**
>
> Encourage the children to use a combination of free-hand drawing and cookie cutter printing to create great designs.

Suggested activities and discussions

▶ Encourage the children to create their own wearable art. Use the method as outlined above, but use fabric paint and place the printing block onto the garment, cover with scrap paper then roller over. Note: it is advisable to wash and iron clothing before decorating it!

▶ Create a landscape by encouraging each child to create a house, tree, car, post box etc., or perhaps a lighthouse, ships and freestanding rocks. The fantastic thing with this process is you can draw onto the Styrofoam sheet then cut around the drawing and print it, so entire scenes can be created.

▶ If you don't plan to use the printing blocks again then turn them into a word of art. Whilst the paint is still wet, sprinkle with glitter or confetti. Alternatively allow the paint to dry then attach embellishments using PVA glue.

▶ Using thin paper and chalks it is possible to produce a delicate rubbing from your Styrofoam printing block. To prevent the chalk from coming off, seal with a fixing spray when the rubbing is complete.

Useful links for additional resources

www.bbc.co.uk/learningzone/clips: type '7733' in the search engine for a step-by-step video of the process.

www.happinessishomemade.net: type 'printing' in search field for a list of more ideas.

Felt or foam printing

There is a huge range of pre-cut felt and fun foam shapes that are ideal for using for printing. If you are unable to source shapes then simply grab some craft felt and cut your own!

What you need:

- ▶ Thick card (mount board is ideal)
- ▶ Pre-cut felt/foam shapes, or felt/foam sheets
- ▶ Scissors
- ▶ PVA glue and glue spreaders
- ▶ Poster paints or printing inks
- ▶ Rollers and paint trays
- ▶ Coloured or white A4 paper

What you do:

1. If you are using pre-cut shapes allow the children to pick their own then place the shapes on the board either as a pattern or as a picture.
2. If you are using sheets then encourage the children to cut out the shapes they require.
3. Once they are happy with the design or picture, stick the shapes on the card.

4. Cover the entire design, including the card, with a thin layer of PVA glue and allow to dry.

5. When completely dry, pour a little paint into the tray and roller back and forth.

6. Roller the paint onto the surface of the block, ensuring the felt/foam pieces are given a thin, even coating.

7. Place a piece of paper on top of the block and rub gently over the surface with your hands.

8. Gently pull the paper off the block and allow to dry fully.

Tip!

Improve the quality of the finished print by not pushing down hard when rolling back and forth. This will mean only the raised surface is covered in paint, and not the background.

Suggested activities and discussions

▶ Use works of art such as 'The Snail' by Henri Matisse or 'Succession' by Wassily Kandinsky to inspire the children to create their own masterpieces.

▶ It is possible to obtain letters as well as shapes; encourage the children to create banners, or gift cards with messages. Note: stick the letters on backwards, so when printed they read the correct way round!

▶ Encourage the children to look at repeat patterns and make their own. You could discuss simple repeat patterns such as a brick wall, railings or a zebra crossing. They can make the repeat pattern on their block, or else simply encourage them to print the block several times in rows and columns to create their own repeat patterns.

▶ Once dry, the block can be used to create rubbings. Simply place a piece of thin paper on the block and rub over the surface using a crayon, chalk or soft pencil e.g. 6B.

Useful links for additional resources

www.youtube.com: type 'repeat patterns' in the search engine to find a selection of age-appropriate videos that discuss repeat patterns.

Health and safety tips

▶ Whilst cutting shapes, ensure children are supervised at all times to reduce the risk of injury.

Toy printing

This technique encourages children to look at the toys they play with in a new light. For example, the tyres on an old toy car leave a great design on a piece of paper!

What you need:

- Selection of toys
- Poster paints in a selection of colours, and paint trays
- Thin flat sponge or paper towel
- Coloured or white A4 paper
- Cereal packets and sticky tape (optional)
- Scissors

What you do:

1. Pour a little paint into the middle of the sponge, fold in half and gently squeeze to disperse the paint evenly.
2. Place the sponge in the tray.
3. Gently press the chosen toy into the paint-covered sponge, moving the toy.
4. Press the toy onto the paper. If using a toy with moving parts, for example a pull-back friction car, place on the paper and allow the car to make its own tracks.

5. If you are using things that move or roll such as marbles then cut the side out of a cereal packet (seal the ends if needed). Place some paper in the bottom and roll the toys around so they leave trails.

Suggested activities and discussions

▶ Encourage the children to experiment with this technique. For example, plastic building bricks create printing blocks, while an unstuffed teddy or soft toy can make interesting prints!

▶ Items such as dice and dominoes also make good printing blocks, and provide the opportunity to discuss numbers; perhaps print a game of dominoes as you play.

▶ If you are using dolls, talk about body parts and how we leave our own prints in the form of fingerprints or footprints, e.g. in the sand.

▶ Why not make a game of it? Encourage each child to cover the wheels of a toy car with paint, then see how long a trail they can make without renewing the paint. The longest trail wins!

Useful links for additional resources

www.rainydaymum.co.uk: type 'print' into the search field for a range of further ideas.

http://creativeconnectionsforkids.com: type 'critter painting' into the search field for instructions on painting with sensory toys.

www.artfulparent.com: type 'print making' into the search field for ideas for all types of printing.

Printing with found objects

Once you start looking, you'll be amazed at the free and found items you can utilise for your printing. You'll soon find yourself looking at something and wondering about the ways you can use it!

What you need:

▶ Selection of items, e.g. bolts, screws, corks, plastic bottles, bubble pack, corrugated card, etc.

▶ Flat paint trays

▶ Thin flat sponges

▶ Poster paints or similar in a selection of colours

▶ Coloured or white A4 paper

What you do:

1. Pour a little paint on the sponge, fold in half and squash to disperse the paint.
2. Place the sponge in the tray.
3. Tap your chosen item on to the sponge, so it picks up a thin layer of paint.
4. Press the paint-covered surface onto the paper to create your print.

Suggested activities and discussions

▶ Encourage the children to create their own piece of artwork. They can make random patterns or create an entire image using the different found items.

▶ Look at shape and size of items such as bolts and screws. Encourage the children to print the smallest to the largest. Ask how many sides the shape has; perhaps experiment with creating simple repeat patterns.

▶ If you use fabric paint, the children can be encouraged to print on calico bags or aprons, which they can use themselves or give as gifts.

▶ Any thin item can be used to create rubbings, for example, keys, flat buttons, coins, etc. Simply place under a sheet of paper and rub over with a crayon or chalk.

Useful links for additional resources

http://picklebums.com: click on 'activities for kids', then type 'printing' into the search field for additional information and ideas.

www.cbc.ca/parents/index.html: type 'corduroy' into the search field then click on the first result for a step-by-step on how to make fabric stamps.

www.growingajeweledrose.com: type 'printing' into the search field for more ideas.

Health and safety tips

▶ When using found items, ensure they are cleaned well before use.

Tile printing

Although you can only produce one print from this process, it is a very tactile form of printing and offers opportunities for various discussions with the children as they work.

What you need:

- ► Smooth ceramic tiles
- ► Poster paints or similar, in various colours
- ► Cotton buds
- ► Rollers
- ► Coloured or white A4 paper

Tip!

If you cannot source ceramic tiles then stick an A4 plastic sleeve to a table with tape and use this.

What you do:

1. Pour a little paint onto the surface of the tile, then roller back and forth to create a thin, even layer of paint.

2. Using the cotton buds, allow the children to draw an image or make a pattern. If they prefer they can use their fingertips.

3. Take a piece of paper and carefully lay it over the top of the paint.

4. Gently rub over the entire piece of paper, trying to ensure that the paper does not move as you work.

5. Slowly pull the paper back to reveal the print, and place to one side to allow it to dry.

Suggested activities and discussions

▶ Once the designs are dry, laminate them so they can be used as place mats. If the designs are small or can be cut up they can be laminated and used as coasters.

▶ Encourage the children to draw themselves or one another. When the prints are dry, cut them out and use them to create a friendship chain. As the children draw, discuss what it is to be a friend, how they treat friends, how they can support their friends, etc.

▶ Encourage the children to experiment by overlaying or blending colours. You can discuss what happens with colours when they are mixed. These experiments can be embellished with other printing techniques such as cookie cutter printing or Styrofoam printing.

Useful links for additional resources

www.artfulparent.com: type 'printmaking' into the search field for a range of ideas.

http://childhood101.com: type 'printing' into the search field for a list of printing-related blog posts.

Sponge printing

Sponges are inexpensive, easy to obtain, available in a large number of designs and are great for using to create fun prints.

What you need:

▶ A selection of shaped sponges
▶ Poster paints or similar, in a range of colours
▶ Flat paint trays
▶ Coloured or white A4 paper

What you do:

1. Pour a little paint into the tray and allow it to settle.
2. Gently dab the sponge onto the paint.
3. When the sponge has an even layer of paint, press onto the paper to make the print.
4. Once the design is complete, place it to one side to allow it to dry.

Suggested activities and discussions

▶ Encourage the children to create a mirror print. This is achieved by decorating the top half of the piece of paper. When they have finished printing, fold the paper in half. Gently rub over the surface then open out to reveal the mirror print.

▶ Encourage the children to create a rainbow. Load several small sponges with different colours. Then, one at a time, drag the sponge in an arch, placing one colour just above the next. As the children work, encourage them to name the colours and perhaps discuss how a rainbow is created.

▶ Look at lighter and darker colours. Start by printing the lightest colours then work through to the darker colours. Alternately, look at shades by picking a colour then adding a little white or black and printing squares in a line.

▶ Encourage the children to blend their own colours by overlaying the sponges. What do they get if they first dab yellow, then dab blue over the top? For older children, perhaps talk about primary and secondary colours. You could also encourage them to create their own colour wheel.

Useful links for additional resources

www.athomewithali.net: type 'printing' into the search field for a list of techniques and ideas.

Health and safety tips

▶ If the children are cutting their own shapes ensure there is adult supervision at all times.

Play dough printing

Play dough can of course be purchased, but to reduce costs why not have a go at making your own? It makes a printing block and encourages the children to enjoy sensory play.

What you need:

- ▶ Play dough
- ▶ Items to press into the dough, e.g. cookie cutters, rotary pastry cutters, plastic toys, etc.
- ▶ Rolling pins
- ▶ Poster paints or printing inks
- ▶ Rollers and flat paint trays
- ▶ Plastic knives
- ▶ Coloured or white A4 paper
- ▶ Thin wooden batons
- ▶ PVA glue and glue spreaders

What you do:

1. Place the batons either side of the ball of dough, and roll out until the rolling pin hits the batons.
2. Use the batons to trim the dough into a square or rectangle.

3. Push the items into the dough to create a pattern or picture.

4. Allow the dough to dry out, then cover with a thin layer of PVA glue and allow the glue to dry.

5. Once dry, cover with a thin layer of paint then place the paper over the top.

6. Gently rub over the surface to ensure all of the paper comes into contact with the paint.

7. Carefully pull back the paper to reveal the completed print.

8. Place the print to one side to allow it to dry.

Suggested activities and discussions

▶ As the children work with the play dough, encourage them to discuss how it feels, and how it acts when they roll it out. Ask them questions such as: how hard do they have to press into it to make a mark? How hard to they have to pull on the tool to get it out of the dough? Is it warm or cold to the touch?

▶ Encourage the children to look at texture by experimenting with different items. These could include lace, fabric, netting (the type fruit is packed in), leaves, chains and combs.

▶ Combine this technique with making quick and simple hanging decorations. Rather than allowing the dough to dry before using it, use whilst still pliable. When the prints have been created, use a cookie cutter to cut out shapes from the textured dough. Finally, use a straw to create a hole in the top of each decoration, sprinkle with glitter and allow to dry.

Useful links for additional resources

www.blogmemom.com: type 'print' into the search field for a list of ideas.

www.learning4kids.net: type 'print' or 'printing' into the search field for further inspiration.

Health and safety tips

▶ If using any items that have a sharp edge, ensure adult supervision at all times.

▶ When using dough with young children, dissuade them from putting it into their mouths.

Glue printing

Glue may not be the first thing that springs to mind when you want to do some printing – but it is in fact an inexpensive medium for creating your own printing block. The bonus with this technique is you can use the block time and time again, allowing you to repeat the process in future sessions.

What you need:

▶ Thick card or mount board

▶ PVA glue in a bottle with a nozzle

▶ Poster paints or similar, in various colours

▶ Rollers and flat paint trays

▶ Pencils

▶ Coloured or white A4 paper

What you do:

1. Encourage the children to draw a simple design or picture on the card.

2. When they are happy with their design, follow the pencil lines with the glue.

3. Once the lines have been 'traced' with the glue, place the block to one side to allow to completely dry (overnight if possible).

4. When it is fully dry and the glue has hardened, place a little paint into the tray then roller back and forth to cover the roller with a thin and even layer of paint.

5. Apply the paint to the glue block, trying not to cover the background as well.

6. Take a piece of paper and place over the block. Gently rub over the surface of the paper.

7. Carefully peel back to reveal the print created and place to one side to allow it to dry.

Suggested activities and discussions

► As the children create their designs, encourage them to discuss how the glue comes out of the bottle. If they squeeze gently does a lot or a little come out? If they squeeze hard, does more or less come out? Is it easier to create a straight, a curved or a wiggly line?

► If you decide not to use the blocks again then turn them into works of art.

Allow the paint to dry, cover with a thin layer of glue, sprinkle with glitter and add further decorations such as feathers, pompoms, stickers, etc.

► Rather than use card as the basis for the block use a piece of acetate. Once the printing process is complete it can be turned into a light catcher by framing with a piece of card and placing in the window. Note: you will need to experiment to find a paint that dries well on the acetate.

► Because of the raised surface, these blocks can also be used to create rubbings. Simply place a piece of paper over the surface (when the paint is dry) and rub a crayon over the surface. If you find the paper moves as you work, use large paperclips, small bulldog clips or pegs to hold it in place.

Useful links for additional resources

www.thechocolatemuffintree.com: type 'glue print' into the search field for a photographic step-by-step.

www.thislittleproject.com: type 'doodle rubbings' into the search field.

www.messforless.net: type 'hot glue' into the search field for step-by-step instructions on how to use a glue gun for rubbings.

Paint roller printing

This is a fun method that allows you to print large areas in one go. There are two methods covered, and with both you never really know what you will end up with until you make your first print!

What you need:

- ▶ Foam rollers (method one)
- ▶ Elastic bands or string (method one)
- ▶ Rolling pins (method two)
- ▶ Foam shapes (method two)
- ▶ PVA glue (method two)
- ▶ Poster paints or similar, in various colours
- ▶ Flat paint trays or a sheet of perspex
- ▶ Coloured or white A4 paper

What you do:

Method one

1. Tightly wrap elastic bands or string around the foam roller, so they make an indent in the roller.
2. Pour paint into the flat tray then roller back and forth so the roller has an even covering of paint.

3. Roller in one long continuous movement on the paper to transfer the design onto the paper.

4. Repeat the process as many times you want!

Method two

1. Attach foam shapes to the rolling pin using the glue.

2. Once you are happy the rolling pin has enough shapes in place, pour paint into the flat tray.

3. Roller back and forth, so the roller has an even covering of paint.

4. Roller in one long continuous movement onto the paper to transfer the design.

5. Again, repeat the process as many times as you want.

Suggested activities and discussions

▶ Encourage the children to experiment with blending colours by placing one or two different colours in the tray. As they roller back and forth, the colours will blend on the roller. When they roll the design onto the paper they can see the new colours that have been created.

▶ Create wrapping paper for gifts and backing paper for other projects. For larger projects use lining paper, which is inexpensive and easy to obtain.

▶ Why not use fabric paint for this technique and create your own 'designer' fabric? Medium weight cotton or calico is ideal. This can be used for simple sewing projects.

▶ Experiment with the design by rolling the rolling pin one way, then overlay a second design by rolling it in a different direction.

Tip!

When using fabric, wash it before printing on it to remove any 'dressing' in the fabric.

Useful links for additional resources

www.handmadecharlotte.com: type 'roller printing' into the search field for a clever alternative method.

http://the-joy-of-my-life-and-other-things.blogspot.co.uk: type 'printing' into the search field for a selection of other ideas and techniques.

www.artful-child.com: type 'roller painting' into the search field for a step-by-step guide.

Bubble printing

Kids love bubbles, so they're sure to love this technique that involves blowing mountains of bubbles using a straw!

What you need:

- Washing-up liquid
- Shallow trays
- Inks or food dyes
- Straws
- White A4 paper

What you do:

1. Fill the tray with approximately 2.5cm (1") of water, then add one tablespoon of washing-up liquid. Add as much ink/food dye as needed to make a dark colour. Mix well.
2. Place the straw into the liquid and blow down it. Keep blowing until there is a large mound of bubbles.
3. Remove the straw then carefully place the paper on top of the bubbles.
4. Gently lower the paper so the bubbles burst.
5. Stop lowering the paper when you are just short of the tray's sides, to avoid obtaining a straight line on your print.

6. Once most of the bubbles have burst, lift the paper, place it face-up and allow it to dry.

7. Repeat the process as many times as you want.

Tip!

▶ Colours can be layered over one another. Simply allow the paper to dry, change the colour and repeat the process.

▶ It is better to start with the lightest colour and work to the darkest colour.

Suggested activities and discussions

▶ As the children work, discuss how bubbles are made and ask them what other activities involve bubbles. Also talk to them about bubbles in nature, e.g. sea foam.

▶ This technique is great for creating backgrounds such as underwater scenes. It could also be teamed with story time, poetry or rhyme time. For example, encourage the children to create a scene from the 'Five Little Fishes' rhyme.

▶ Rather than bubble printing on paper, use thin card and then use it to make bookmarks, greetings cards, simple gift boxes, covers for books, etc.

Useful links for additional resources

www.sciencekids.co.nz: type 'bubbles' into the search field for related activities.

www.imcpl.org: type 'bubbles' in the search field for information and activities.

http://babyparenting.about.com: type 'bubbles' into the search field for bubble-related features.

http://artful-kids.com/blog: type 'bubbles' into the search field for additional ways to paint with bubbles.

Health and safety tips

▶ Prior to trying this technique, ensure you talk to the children about the importance of blowing down the straw rather than sucking up from it.

▶ To reduce the risk of putting the soapy end of the straw in their mouths, mark one end (or use bendy straws) so the children do not get confused which end is which.

Simple screen-printing

This is a simplified version of the process used by many printers, and can be used to print on a wide range of different mediums.

What you need:

▶ Foam core
▶ Screen printing fabric
▶ Squeegees
▶ Craft knives
▶ Poster paints or inks
▶ Staplers
▶ Self-adhesive paper
▶ Coloured or white A4 paper
▶ Pencils
▶ Scissors
▶ Masking tape

What you do:

1. Cut a frame out of the foam core, making the window slightly larger than the print you want to make.
2. Cut the fabric so it is slightly larger than the total size of the foam core.
3. Stretch the fabric around the foam core and staple in place, ensuring the fabric is stretched tight.
4. Cut the self-adhesive paper slightly smaller than the window of the frame.
5. Encourage the children to draw a design made up of simple shapes or silhouettes.
6. Using a craft knife (suggested adult step), cut out the shapes so they become holes in the paper.
7. Peel off the protective layer on the paper and attach the paper on the underside of the fabric, positioning it inside the window.
8. On the inside of the window (core side up), place masking tape around the outside so it slightly overlaps the self-adhesive paper but does not cut off any of the design.
10 Place the printing screen onto the paper/fabric and place a paint/ink along one edge on the inside of the frame.
11. Whilst holding in place, use the squeegee to spread the paint from one side to the other in one simple movement.
12. Repeat this process a couple of times to ensure the paint/ink has gone through the holes.
13. Carefully lift the frame to reveal the print on the paper/fabric.
14. Place the print to one side to dry, and repeat this process as many times as you want.

Tip!

▶ The design can be reversed and you can stick shapes onto the fabric, so that the background of the design is printed rather than the design.

▶ The paper design will start to lift after several prints have been created. At this time peel off the paper and throw it away.

▶ The frame can be used again if the fabric is washed and allowed to dry.

Suggested activities and discussions

▶ Encourage the children to decorate simple white T-shirts. These can be used to raise funds for a special project or given as gifts. In order to avoid the print going through to the back of the T-shirt, place a piece of plastic between both layers.

▶ Obtain some pre-made calico or medium-weight cotton bags. Screen print onto them and allow the design to dry. Once dry, encourage the children to embellish further with simple hand stitching, or use fabric pens to 'work up' the designs further.

▶ Tie this technique in with another topic, for example, going green or road safety. Encourage the children to create posters that can be used to share the new knowledge they have gained.

Useful links for additional resources

http://onegoldenapple.blogspot.co.uk: type ' silk' into the search field for step-by-step instructions with images.

www.parents.com: type 'screen printing' into the search field.

www.squidoo.com: type 'children make prints' into the search field for step-by-step instructions for different printing techniques, including screen printing.

Fingerprints

This activity can be used either as a stand-alone activity or as a bolt-on to the hand and foot printing section. Taking prints of fingers and thumbs is very simple but can open up a world of inspiration, ideas and discussions.

What you need:

▶ Non-toxic inkpads in various colours

▶ Paper or other suitable surface

▶ Fine-line black pen (black biro)

What you do:

1. Gently press the pads of fingers or thumbs onto the inkpad.
2. Press each ink-covered finger or thumb onto the paper to create the print.

Suggested activities and discussions

▶ Encourage the children to create some fun art with their finger and thumb prints by embellishing or drawing elements onto the prints, such as a face, legs and arms. For ideas, visit the websites suggested below. As the children work, you could discuss what makes their fingerprints different from their families' and friends'. You could talk about paw prints created by cats and dogs; although these animals do not have the finger print patterns on their paws like humans have, they do leave different prints from one another (size and shape).

▶ Link finger and thumb printing with story or rhyme time. For example, perhaps encourage the children to create a fingerprint painting of the Very Hungry Caterpillar and the fruit he eats (apple, pear, plumb, strawberry and orange). Other stories you could explore and link to could include 'The Three Little Pigs' and 'Tadpole's Promise'. Alternatively, link to rhymes, for example 'Three Little Fishes', 'Baby Bumble Bee', 'Two Little Dickie Birds' and 'Ladybird, Ladybird'.

▶ Why not encourage the children to play 'detective' by placing fingerprints (without the ink) on a glass or a balloon? They can then 'dust' for prints by following the instructions on the free downloadable PDF listed in the resources below. You could also encourage the children to take each other's fingerprints using a homemade finger print card as part of themed play.

▶ Create a special necklace by pressing two thumbprints (in the shape of a heart) into polymer clay. Simply roll out a small ball of polymer clay so it's approximately 5mm thick. Press the thumb twice into the clay to create a heart shape then use a small cookie cutter to cut around it. Add a hole at the top with a cocktail stick or similar then bake as per manufacturers instructions. Once cool, place onto a piece of decorative cord or a chain.

Useful links for additional resources

www.squidoo.com/thumbprint_characters: full of ideas for turning finger and thumb prints into different pictures

'Ed Emberley's Fingerprint Drawing Book': plenty more ideas for fun and easy art

images.birthdayinabox.com/partyplanning/fingerprintart.pdf: brilliantly simple finger print ideas

kids4crafts.blogspot.co.uk/2009/03/fingerprint-bugs.html: even more ideas for turning finger and thumb prints into art

www.kidsciencechallenge.com/pdfs/2009activities/KSC_Fingerprint_2009.pdf: free PDF containing instructions for dusting fingerprints!

Rubber stamp printing

Printing with rubber stamps, whether they are mounted on wood, foam or acrylic, is a great way of introducing children to almost any topic or theme. There are many simple techniques that can be employed and the stamps can be used on an array of materials, including paper, card, wood, fabric and polymer clay.

What you need:

▶ Rubber stamps
▶ Foam inkpads
▶ A suitable surface

What you do:

1. Ink the stamp evenly, by dabbing the stamp onto the inkpad.
2. Hover the stamp over your project, just above the required position.
3. Position the stamp face-down and press evenly, making sure the entire stamp comes into contact with the surface.

4. Pull the stamp up vertically, making sure you do not smudge the image.

5. Embellish the image as dictated by your chosen project.

Tip!

► Inkpads come in a variety of different inks that have slightly different uses:

  ▷ Pigment ink is a slow-drying ink. While it dries it is easily smudged and may bleed if used with water-based paint, so allow it to dry fully.

  ▷ Dye ink is a fast-drying ink and some makes are also water resistant, allowing you to paint over them using water-based paints.

  ▷ Embossing ink can be obtained as a clear or a coloured ink, and is slow-drying. It is ideal for an array of different crafting techniques (one is outlined below).

  ▷ Fabric ink is ideal for stamping on plain clothing such as old t-shirts, and can be 'set' with a hot iron (adult step).

► If the ink appears to have dried a little on the surface of the stamp then breathe heavily on the surface and the ink should 'liven' up.

► Once you have finished the activity you will need to clean your stamps.

  The easiest method is to use baby wipes or a damp cloth and gently wipe the surface of the stamp to remove the ink.

► To keep your stamps in good condition, store in a box – rubber side up – in a dry place. If storing more than one layer deep, place bubble wrap between each layer.

Suggested activities and discussions

► The benefit of using rubber stamps is you can use them again and again, allowing the children to print multiples of the same image. Therefore why not use them to explore and discuss numbers (addition, increasing numbers, odd and even numbers).

► Pick themed stamps to create a mobile. Simply stamp onto thin card, render, then cut out. Create a hole in the top of each using a hole punch, then thread with yarn. Hang the stamps from a coat hanger or alternatively bind some chopsticks (or similar) into a cross, then hang the motifs from the four 'arms'.

► Using a clear pigment ink, stamp onto a suitable surface such as paper or card. Then dab a cotton wool ball into a small amount of craft chalk dust and gently rub over the clear stamped image with the chalk-covered cotton wool, and watch the image appear as the chalk adheres to the ink. As the children work, encourage them to colour blend and discuss darker and lighter colours or primary and secondary colours. Perhaps explore the theme of magic, or discuss things that are invisible, such as air.

▶ Rubber stamps are great for creating projects such a homemade dominoes, snap cards and dice.

▶ If your stamps are fairly flat then they are also ideal to use to create rubbings. Simply place on a smooth surface face-up, position a piece of thin paper over the top, then use pencils or crayons to create your design.

Useful links for additional resources

http://randomcreative.hubpages.com: type 'rubber stamps' into the search field for further ideas. Includes suggestions on how to make your own stamps.

www.buzzfeed.com/pippa/diy-stamp-projects: although many of these projects are aimed at adults, many can be adapted to suit children.

www.sewmamasew.com: type 'rubber stamping' into the search field for step-by-step instructions on how to make your own stamps (ideal for older children and those with good hand-eye co-ordination).

http://en.wikipedia.org/wiki/List_of_animal_names: contains the names for male, female, young and groups of animals.

www.firstpalette.com/tool_box/printables/cube.html: downloadable dice template.

Health and safety tips

▶ Although most inks are now non-toxic, always try to keep an eye on children as they work to ensure they do not put ink-covered fingers or tools in their mouths.

Spaghetti printing

This is a fun use for an every day food and the kids will love the effects they can achieve when printing with spaghetti or any other pasta you have to hand.

What you need:

► Spaghetti or other pasta
► Water-soluble colour (paint, food dye or inks)
► Rubber gloves
► Apron
► Plenty of newspaper to cover work surface
► A4 paper
► Bowls

What you do:

Method one

1. Cook the spaghetti and allow it to cool completely before using.
2. Place a handful of the cooked spaghetti into a bowl and add a few drops of your chosen colour.

3. Mix the colour and the spaghetti until the spaghetti is covered.
4. Place the spaghetti onto paper then place another piece of paper on top.
5. Gently rub over the surface, so the paper comes into contact with the spaghetti.
6. Carefully peel the paper back to discover your finished print.
7. Place to one side and allow to dry naturally.
8. If you wish to build up the design then repeat the process once the previous layer has dried.

Method two

1. Cook the spaghetti and allow it to cool completely before using.
2. Place a handful of the cooked spaghetti into a bowl and add a few drops of your chosen colour.
3. Mix the colour and the spaghetti until the spaghetti is covered.
4. Pick up at handful of spaghetti and drop onto the paper.
5. Remove and drop again covering the entire surface.
6. If you want crisp lines do not push the spaghetti around, just pick straight up. However if you want a different effect push the spaghetti around.
7. Put to one side and allow to dry naturally.
8. If you wish to build up the design then repeat the process once the previous layer has dried.

Tip!

▶ The added bonus with method one is if the spaghetti is carefully removed from the first piece of paper you have two prints for the price of one.

▶ If you are going to build up several layers of colour then start with the darkest first.

Suggested activities and discussions

▶ As you work why not discuss where spaghetti/pasta comes from. How is it made? Which country does it originate from? Ask if they like spaghetti/pasta? If so, what is their favourite?

- ▶ Look at artists such as Jackson Pollock and Janet Sobel and encourage the children to look at their work and how they can use this as inspiration for their own spaghetti/pasta art.
- ▶ Explore this process by using different shapes/types of pasta (cartwheels, bows and shells) and discuss the difference marks each pasta type creates. If using spaghetti, use full lengths and see what results can be achieved. As they curl the spaghetti discuss the shapes that are created. Then encourage the children to cut the spaghetti into shorter lengths, so they can discover what difference this makes to the marks create. As they experiment, discuss terms such as length and making things shorter and shorter still.

Useful links for additional resources

www.jacksonpollock.org: front page includes a 'canvas' that can be used to create a Jackson Pollock style picture.

www.jackson-pollock.org: full biography and images of art.

www.haberarts.com/sobel.htm: brief introduction to Janet Sobel's work.

Health and safety tips

- ▶ If you are working with children likely to put items into their mouths then ensure the colourings you use are non-toxic e.g. food dyes.
- ▶ Always check for food intolerances/allergies before using food-based items for craft activities.

Sun printing

This is completely different from the other types of printing we've covered in this book, as it relies on a chemical process and the power of the sun. It will open up a world of fun, activities and discussions on a sunny day!

What you need:

Method one

▶ Sunprint paper

▶ Acrylic sheet

▶ Cardboard

▶ Piece of dark, thick cloth

▶ Bowl of water

▶ Objects to use for printing

▶ Paper towel

▶ Room that receives no direct sunlight

Method two

▶ Light-sensitive dye

▶ Fabric, wood or other natural material

- Paper plate
- Sponge spreader
- Washing machine
- Washing powder
- Plastic tablecloth
- A frame made from stiff card
- Painters/masking tape
- Stencil or interesting items
- Acrylic sheet

What you do:

Method one

1. Working in the room that receives no direct sunlight place the sunprint paper on the piece of card and arrange the objects you are going to print onto it.

2. Place the acrylic sheet over the top, this holds the items in place and flattens them.

3. Place the piece of cloth over the top and carefully take everything outside into the sun.

4. Remove the cover and watch the paper turn white. When almost all of the blue has disappeared your print is complete.

5. Remove the acrylic sheet and objects then place the sunprint paper into the bowl of water to rinse. As you rinse the white paper will turn blue and the lue will turn white.

6. Leave the paper in the water for up to five minutes (or as per manufacturers instructions).

7. Place the print onto a couple of sheets of paper towel and allow to dry naturally.

Tip!

- This process can be done on a cloudy day however the printing process will take a little longer, up to 20 minutes.

- Try to use flat items such as lace, feathers, pressed grasses etc. as these produce crisper results. If the items do not lie flat then the suns rays can 'sneak' under the edges and create softer edges to the finished print.

Method two

1. Cover your work surface with the tablecloth and place some dye onto a paper plate.
2. Lay your fabric/wood etc. flat then using the tape attach the frame (sticking around the outer edges) where you are going to paint the dye.
3. Evenly spread a thin layer of dye over the surface inside the frame and then remove the frame.
4. Whilst the dye is still damp lay your stencil or objects in place.
5. Place the acrylic sheet over the top then place in direct sunlight.
6. Watch as the colours of the dye change, this can take 5 – 20 minutes (consult manufacturers instructions).
7. Once the process is complete remove the acrylic sheet and the objects then wash in a washing machine to remove the dye.

Tip!

▶ The dye is fairly clear when you first paint it on; it is the process of placing in the sun that darkens it.

▶ Print a negative (perhaps from a photograph) onto an overhead acrylic sheet to create a 'stencil' for your project.

▶ If the surface of the project is wet then blot using tissue paper so it is damp for improved results.

▶ If your are printing on an item such as a T-shirt then place a piece of card wrapped in plastic between the layers, so the dye does not penetrate both layers.

▶ Always follow the manufacturers instructions if different from the above.

Suggested activities and discussions

▶ As you watch the sun-print form, why not discuss what is happening; that the ultraviolet rays from the sun are creating a chemical reaction. This could be linked to how the sun creates 'food' in plants via the process of photosynthesis. The power of the sun could be discussed further by talking about how water left in the sun can become warm, how the sun can burn our skin and also how the sun can be used to create energy using solar panels.

▶ As you collect items/objects for the printing process explore shape and size. Perhaps look at different leaves and discuss how leaves such as maple have sharp points and are made up predominantly of straight lines whilst leaves from the ash tree are rounded.

▶ Encourage the children to be imaginative when they lay the items onto their project; for example, they could create a 'scene' or a pattern. Perhaps a fern leaf could represent a tree, a daisy could become the sun or a leaf could become the sail on a boat. If they are unable to find the exact shape they need then help them.

▶ If your sun prints have been created on paper, perhaps use the results to create works of art by placing in a frame, or alternatively create greeting cards. If you have created them on fabric then the fabric can be used to make an array of different projects from a simple apron, bag or wall hanging.

Useful links for additional resources

www.youtube.com: type 'lumi workshop' in the search field for a 53-minute video giving step-by-step instructions for using light sensitive dye.

www.naturedetectives.org.uk: contains a leaf identification sheet.

www.fredaldous.co.uk: scroll down to 'blog' then type in 'sun print kit' for a step-by-step blog post.

Health and safety tips

▶ If you are working outside for any length of time, ensure the children have appropriate sun protection (both clothing and lotion).

The Little Books Club

There is always something in Little Books to help and inspire you. Packed full of lovely ideas, Little Books meet the need for exciting and practical activities that are fun to do, address the Early Learning Goals and can be followed in most settings. Everyone is a winner!

We publish 5 new Little Books a year. Little Books Club members receive each of these 5 books as soon as they are published for a reduced price. The subscription cost is £29.99 – a one off payment that buys the 5 new books for £4.99 instead of £8.99 each.

In addition to this, Little Books Club Members receive:
· Free postage and packing on anything ordered from the Featherstone catalogue
· A 15% discount voucher upon joining which can be used to buy any number of books from the Featherstone catalogue
· Members price of £4.99 on any additional Little Book purchased
· A regular, free newsletter dealing with club news, special offers and aspects of Early Years curriculum and practice
· All new Little Books on approval - return in good condition within 30 days and we'll refund the cost to your club account

Call 020 7458 0200 or email: littlebooks@bloomsbury.com for an enrolment pack. Or download an application form from our website:
www.bloomsbury.com

The **Little Books** series consists of:

50
All through the year
Bags, Boxes & Trays
Big Projects
Bricks & Boxes
Celebrations
Christmas
Circle Time
Clay and Malleable Materials
Clothes and Fabric
Colour, Shape and Number
Cooking from Stories
Cooking Together
Counting
Dance
Dance Music CD
Dens
Discovery Bottles
Dough
Drama from Stories
Explorations
Fine Motor Skills
Free and Found
Fun on a Shoestring
Games with Sounds
Gross Motor Skills
Growing Things
ICT
Investigations
Junk Music
Kitchen Stuff

Language Fun
Light and Shadow
Listening
Living Things
Look and Listen
Making Books and Cards
Making Poetry
Maps and Plans
Mark Making
Maths Activities
Maths from Stories
Maths Outdoors
Maths Problem Solving
Maths Songs and Games
Messy Play
Minibeast Hotels
Multi-sensory Stories
Music
Nursery Rhymes
Opposites
Outdoor Play
Outside in All Weathers
Painting
Parachute Play
Persona Dolls
Phonics
Playground Games
Prop Boxes for Role Play
Props for Writing
Puppet Making
Puppets in Stories

Resistant Materials
Rhythm and Raps
Role Play
Role Play Windows
Sand and Water
Science through Art
Scissor Skills
Seasons
Sequencing Skills
Sewing and Weaving
Small World Play
Sound Ideas
Special Days
Stories from around the
world
Story bags
Storyboards
Storybuilding
Storytelling
Time and Money
Time and Place
Topsy Turvy
Traditional Tales
Treasure Baskets
Treasure Boxes
Tuff Spot Activities
Washing lines
Woodwork
Writing

All available from
www.bloomsbury.com/featherstone